The W

The Unofficial Biography

By Christian Guiltenane

SUNBIRD

Published by Ladybird Books Ltd 2010
A Penguin Company
Penguin Books Ltd, 80 Strand, London, WC2R 0RL, UK
Penguin Books Australia Ltd, Camberwell, Victoria, Australia
Penguin Group (NZ), 67 Apollo Drive, Rosedale, North Shore
0632, New Zealand (a division of Pearson New Zealand Ltd)

Sunbird is a trade mark of Ladybird Books Ltd

All rights reserved. No part of this publication may be reproduced,
stored in a retrieval system, or transmitted in any form or by any means,
electronic, mechanical, photocopying, recording or otherwise,
without the prior consent of the copyright owner.

The publisher does not have any control over and does not assume any responsibility
for author or third-party websites or their content.
Written by Christian Guiltenane
Photo credits: Cover: Photo by Fiona Hanson/Press Association Images.
Insert photos: Pages 16, 30, 44 and 68 by Fiona Hanson/Press Association Images.
Page 56 by Suzan/Press Association Images.
Colour Insert photos: Page 1 by Suzan/Press Association Images.
Page 2; Siva by Fiona Hanson/Press Association, Nathan by Suzan/Press Association,
Jay by Nigel French/Press Association Images Images.
Pages 3 and 7 by Suzan/Press Association Images.
Pages 4, 5, 6 and 8 by Fiona Hanson/Press Association Images
Copyright © 2010 by Ladybird. All rights reserved.

www.ladybird.com

ISBN: 978-1-40939-067-1

001 - 10 9 8 7 6 5 4 3 2 1

Printed in Great Britain

Contents

Intro	5
How it all began...	12
GETTING TO KNOW...	
Jay McGuiness	16
Max George	30
Nathan Sykes	44
Siva Kaneswaran	56
Tom Parker	68
Coming Together	73
The Road to Success	78
All time low	83
The Album	92
THE FUTURE OF THE WANTED:	
What the experts say	97
Boybands that everybody should know about	110
Who will rival The Wanted?	124

Intro...
Summertime Ball, June, 2010

As the five hunky boys from The Wanted slowly made their way through the winding corridors of Wembley Stadium toward the stage, they could feel butterflies begin to whirl ferociously around in their tightly muscled tums. 'Oh my God,' cutesome Nathan Sykes muttered to his mates, wiping away a bead of sweat. 'I'm so nervous!'

The others, all stern faced but still devilishly handsome, patted him warmly on the back and tried to muster smiles to reassure their troubled pal that everything would be alright. But deep down, they too were feeling just as uneasy, knowing that within a matter of minutes they would be up on stage performing to over 70,000 people.

But getting up and entertaining thousands of people was what the boys had been dreaming about for so long. Right from that warm September day in 2009 when The Wanted was formed, Max, Nathan, Tom, Jay and Siva were determined to make the band as successful as possible; to take on hugely popular boybands like Take That and JLS and give them a run for their money. And in order to do that they knew they had to produce the best songs around to win over as many fans as was humanly possible. And that meant getting out there and making people sit up and take notice of them.

And so, in the weeks running up to this momentous Capital Summertime Ball show, which would see The Wanted sharing a stage with the likes of such chart stars as Rihanna, Usher, JLS and Cheryl Cole, the boys had played to thousands of kids up and down the country on a special schools tour.

At each one of their intimate assembly hall gigs, the lads had been bricking it with nerves, but in a good way. As a new band, they were unsure about how popular they would prove to be with their unsuspecting and very hard-to-please young audiences. So they took to the stage cautiously, hoping that they'd be able to win over the very demanding crowd. Luckily for them – though not all that surprisingly – the band's amazing good looks, bubbly personalities, great tunes and perfect dance moves were so enthralling and captivating that those lucky kids who got to see them up close and personal fell instantly in love with them, and pledged their enduring support, giving the boys a great deal of much needed confidence.

But playing to around 300 school kids at a time was very different to strutting their stuff in front of 70,000 people who had paid good money to see their favourite artists. At this stage in their blossoming career, The Wanted knew they were still pretty much unknown to most people around the UK, having only played their school gigs, appeared on a couple of TV shows and had their debut single 'All Time Low' played on the radio a few times. As of yet, they still weren't exactly household names, so there was a possibility that when they did eventually walk out on that huge stage, the audience, whose ages would range from pre-teen to grown-ups in their 40s and 50s, would simply stare back at them puzzled, wondering who the hell these delicious young boys all were. And that's what made them even more nervous. To be confronted by kids who were already fans was one thing, but to walk out into the unknown was another, and that had given the boys some sleepless nights.

Hours before they had even arrived at the stadium for their sound check, the nerves had set in. Tom admitted that he had found it hard to get a good night's rest, stirring four or five times during the night. 'I kept waking up and thinking about the gig,' Tom had told his bandmates over breakfast that morning as they waited for their car to come and pick them up. Later, when the boys eventually arrived at the empty stadium for their last minute rehearsal, they all started to feel the nerves.

As they were led to the stage from their dressing room, for the first time, Siva and Jay had covered their eyes. The very idea of them performing a song in a stadium as world famous as Wembley, where superstars like Madonna and Oasis had played to thousands of people, was too much for them to deal with. Even cheeky Max, who normally wouldn't let any nerves get to him, couldn't believe that they were being invited to sing at such an iconic venue. 'We just don't deserve to be here,' he bashfully said, as he and the guys munched on the food and sweets that had been left in their dressing room by the show's organisers. 'This kind of thing just doesn't happen.'

But as they neared the stage, they began to realize that it did happen and was about to happen to them at any minute. As they waited to be called, they could hear the deafening roar of the crowd. They were definitely up for a good time, the boys decided, and fortunately for them and the other artists on the bill, the crowd seemed to welcome everyone who came to the stage with enthusiastic cheers. The boys hoped that the crowd would be just as friendly when they took their spot on stage.

The boys didn't have to wait too long to find out what the tens of thousands of people thought of them, as one of the show's stage managers suddenly stepped forward and ushered them hurriedly up a ramp and onto the stage. As if moving in slow motion, the sight of the crowds packing out the stadium came into the boys' view. At first, the spectacle of seeing 70,000 people packed so tightly together didn't make sense to them, as en masse, the crowd looked like an expanse of material, like a speckled blanket. But as their eyes got used to what they were seeing, they realized that each of those speckles was a single face belonging to a fan who had travelled far and wide to see their favourite artists.

As soon as the boys took their positions, the crowd made it clear that The Wanted were just that – wanted, easing the boys' minds. So when they performed their track 'All Time Low', they did so with gusto and amazing confidence. In what felt like seconds, the song had come to an end, and with it their uneasiness. In its place was a hunger for more. The three and a half minutes they had just experienced had been so exciting; so exhilarating that they had wanted it to last forever. Sadly, it couldn't, mainly because another star was waiting in the wings to get up and perform.

Backstage, the boys fell into a massive affectionate group hug, each so very proud of the other. 'That was the most incredible feeling of my life,' Tom said afterwards. 'I'm not sure which one of us is shaking the most. I just never expected that brilliant reaction.'

Max later admitted he was amazed that he could see most of the crowd singing along with them, but also confessed he was worried that due to his nerves and excitement about being on stage, he might dribble. Luckily, he didn't, even though he felt he was about to.

Back in their dressing room, the boys took a moment to reflect on what had just happened to them, and realized, probably for the first time – but certainly not for the last – that their dreams were beginning to come true: they were fast becoming the UK's most popular and sexiest band!

How it all began...

The summer of 2009 belonged, without a doubt, to the mighty JLS. Just a handful of months after being beaten into second place by Alexandra Burke in a tense X Factor final, the boys were busy flashing their rippling muscles on tour, on the telly and in almost every magazine and newspaper. Around the country, girls were feeling faint as they were struck down with the JLS fever, while thousands of boys-next-door looked on in horror as they realized that if they had to compete with the physical perfection of Marvin, JB, Oritsé and Aston in trying to woo the ladies, they'd have to take more care of themselves and hit the gym pretty smartish!

'Beat Again', the boys' first single, smashed into the number one spot in the month of April. It was swiftly followed by the anthem arm-waver 'Everybody In Love', which became the song of the summer and confirmed the dashing dudes as the boyband of the minute, with no clear rivals set to steal their crown.

But not for long. In a record company building

in the heart of London, a group of musical bigwigs had gathered together to discuss the idea of forming a brand new boyband that would take on JLS and attempt to go one better. This scorching hot combo, they hoped, would be better than the average boybands that had come and gone so quickly before. Oh no, this group would be different. They would be young and edgy, with an air of coolness that no other band had, armed with songs that were a distinct cut above the average, blending pop melodies with indie and R&B sounds.

In these early stages of development, the bigwigs decided that the eventual line-up of boys would work with some of the greatest writers and producers in the world, such as Guy Chambers, the man who wrote 'Angels' for Robbie Williams, dance legend Taio Cruz, and Steve Mac, the very talented guy who wrote and produced many of Westlife's biggest hits. This ambitious plan meant that extra care would have to be taken in choosing the very best talent from around the country. Dealing with talented and important producers like these, the label had to ensure that they found the right collection of boys who were good enough and gifted enough to hack the pace and pull off a great performance. They wanted to find guys who would turn heads, not just with their pretty faces and fantastic bodies, but with amazing vocals and breathtaking dance moves too.

In order to track down only the cream of the boyband crop, the record label bigwigs called upon a casting agent called Jayne Collins, who had previously helped piece together the girl band The Saturdays, to help them with their very special search. And so, in the summer of 2009, Jayne and her team set to work on finding the five members of potentially the greatest boyband in the UK. Maybe even the world!

The journey was a long and hard one. After posting adverts online and in specialist newspapers, Jayne and the record label bods invited hundreds of boys to audition for them, in a similar way to Simon Cowell and Cheryl Cole do on *The X Factor*.

The process was a fascinating one, as it introduced them to some young men who had great voices but sadly didn't fit the look of the band, and some who looked great but whose voices simply didn't match up. The job even got harder when they eventually began to narrow down their search. With a handful of boys in mind, it was up to the team to work out which of them related best to the others. It was all well and good having five hot lads with amazing voices in one band, but it was just as important that the boys all clicked with each other and looked right together. After all, there was nothing worse than a boyband that looked weird, awkward or out of sync with each other up on stage, or in photos.

So eventually, after reauditioning the boys they liked, they settled on five candidates that they felt had what it took to form a boyband like no other. And their names? Max George, Jay McGuiness, Nathan Sykes, Tom Parker and Siva Kaneswaran…

Getting to know...
Jay McGuiness

Age: 20

Date Of Birth: 24/07/90

Hometown: Nottingham

Star Sign: Leo

Favourite Food: Pizza, pasta and pesto, chips, cheese toasties, Starbars, eggs in any form

Height: 6'1"

Eye Colour: Blue

Hair Colour: Brown

Favourite Bands: Coldplay, Newton Faulkner, Florence, Jack Penate, Damien Rice, Justin

Football Team: Celtic, at a push, as he rarely watches footy

Favourite Animal: Chimp, except the one that ate off that woman's face (ate it clean off!)

Favourite TV Show as a Kid: *How 2*: Carol Vorderman, is there anything you didn't teach us?

Recent TV Show: Anything with David Attenborough; in fact he says David Attenborough is his favourite guy right now. And *Misfits*!

Favourite Trainers: Converse

Status: Single

Dream Woman: Vanessa White from The Saturdays

Random Fact: Jay owns a pet lizard – a recent treat after the band hit No1

With his tumbling wavy locks, cute face and wicked sense of humour, Nottingham-born Jay McGuiness is without a doubt a pretty perfect package. Luckily for his fans he's still a single guy. Or so he claims, anyway! But it might come as a surprise to his fans that Jay hasn't always been the wacky fella you all have grown to love. Long, long ago, when the 20 year old star was just a young kid, life was very different. He was forced to suffer a constant stream of ribbing from his schoolmates at All Saints Catholic School in Mansfield, because no matter how hard he tried, he was just pants at football. 'I used to get a bit of stick when I was younger,' he recalls. 'The other kids used to call me banana-kick because I couldn't kick the ball in a straight line.' What made matters worse was that his entire family – his three brothers, one of whom was his twin, sister and mum, who captained the local team – were absolutely crazy about football. So in theory, the love of the sport and skills on the pitch should have been in Jay's blood. But when he actually did set foot on the pitch, it was a whole other story and anyone on the touchlines would be hard-pressed not to snigger at his clutzy ball control. So, whenever his schoolmates were out playing football, Jay would steer well clear, preferring to crash out on the couch at home and watch the telly as he stuffed his face with crisps.

As a result of his dodgy diet, Jay admits that he became something of a porker – and far from the physical beauty he is today.

However, as he pigged out on the couch, eyes glued to Carol Vorderman, little did he know that even though his footwork on the pitch was pretty rubbish, he had hidden skills that would soon come to the fore. And if it hadn't been for his mum injuring herself during a football match, he may never have discovered his true love: dance. Worse still, if it hadn't have been for Mrs McGuiness's mishap, Jay most probably would never have become one fifth of The Wanted, which would ultimately mean that none of us would have had his gorgeous image staring down at us from our bedroom wall.

Because of her untimely injury, Jay's mum decided to take up tap dancing lessons so she could keep fit while she recovered, and brought Jay along for the ride. Although he was a little reluctant at first – after all, if the lads at school teased him about how rubbish he was at football, what would they say about him doing dance classes? – Jay soon got into the swing of things and discovered he had a natural talent for tap. In fact, he realized that he rather liked all kinds of dance and spent much of his spare time throwing shapes to music he heard on the radio. 'It was the only thing I was ever good at,' he remembers. 'I really got obsessed with it.'

But while he was giddy about his new hobby, it wasn't long before he was brought crashing back down to earth when all his supposed mates started teasing him about his new pastime. They branded him Billy Elliott – the light-footed character (from the film of the same name) who has a love for ballet, much to the amusement of his friends and neighbours.

But in spite of the petty jibes that were hurled at poor Jay, he stuck at his dancing and whenever he could he would attend classes and try to perfect his moves. As time went on he realized that his passion for movement was more than just a passing hobby: it was something that he wanted to pursue when he was older. So when he had finished his GCSEs, Jay decided that he wanted to find a place where he could develop his dancing skills even further. He found what he was looking for at the Midlands Dance Academy, affectionately known to the students as MADD. The school was a well respected one, aiming to give its devoted students 'an all round training in order to meet the needs of the Theatre and TV in the 21st century'.

Performers were expected to be able to sing, dance and act, and 'be prepared to use their skills to the maximum in order to secure employment in the performing arts industry.' So far, so *Glee*, you might think. But no! Although the school was full of eager young hopefuls desperate to make it big in the dance world, or in the music industry as a backing dancer, Jay says the school was nothing like the bright and sparkly TV show. Instead, it was all work, work, work. And it was here that young Jay found the confidence to eventually head out into the big wide world to try out for auditions. Sadly for poor Jay, his dream of superstardom remained out of reach as time and time again he rocked up to auditions only to be told on each occasion he hadn't been successful. 'I failed at every one until this, which is lucky. I was going to dance auditions but I was too skinny and geeky.' He added, 'The thing is, I'm not like the other dancers,' he said. 'They were all into R&B and I was into indie and Jack Peñate, Cat Stevens, stuff like that.' Finding it hard to land a job, you could quite easily have expected an eager wannabe like Jay to try an easier route to stardom, by auditioning for something like *The X Factor*, and follow in the footsteps of Shayne Ward, Joe McElderry or Leona Lewis, but for some reason he never got around to it. 'I got quite disheartened from going to auditions and not getting anything so I would have considered [*The X Factor*],' he said, once he'd become a fully fledged member of The Wanted. 'Some of the others did. Tom got kicked out after one round. Max did well with his band Avenue but there was some hoo-ha about them having a manager and they got booted out.'

So bypassing what some would consider a fast route to fame, Jay stuck to the rounds of auditions that he read about in the press or online, or that he'd heard about on the grapevine. Sadly, still no jobs came his way, leaving Jay with no other option but to try out for all manner of alternative dance jobs, even attempting to land a role at the circus. Fortunately for Jay, he was saved from having to dress up as a clown, or whatever misfortune may have befallen him in the big top, as at the very same time he had seen the advert for a boyband and went for that too. Needless to say, we all know which one Jay went for in the end, and we couldn't be happier with his canny choice (though, admittedly, we can't help but as to wonder exactly what kind of get-up poor old Jay would have had to wear as he jumped through hoops or swung on the flying trapeze!).

Chuffed that he had finally made it into a band that looked like it might fare better than ex-X Factor posters, Jay felt confident that he had finally found his calling, and was pleased when he met the other guys who would form the band. He got on with them like a house on fire, and enjoyed hanging out with them at the house in Wandsworth, South London, that they all shared. It was a cosy house; the fridge was well stocked with not-so-healthy beer and pizzas. They spent seven months getting to know each other in-between recording tracks, meeting producers and working out. As time went on, Jay was more and more pleased with the musical direction the band was taking. Instead of crooning wimpy ballads on stools, their songs were a lot more indie influenced, a lot like the music he loved himself. 'I'd say it was edgy pop,' he explained, once he and the boys had recorded several of their delicious tracks. 'But there's a bit of rock and a bit of indie in there too. It's taking a bit of a risk I think; it's certainly not your usual boyband stuff.' He added that when he had first made it into the band, he became a 'total geek' and decided to thoroughly research boybands of the past. He was pleased to discover that The Wanted seemed totally unique. 'I haven't seen one we're similar to,' he boasted. 'Westlife just stand there and sing; we jump around like idiots. We have dance routines but we're not as good as *NSYNC. I think we're a new species of band. Although I might be flattering myself.'

When the Nottingham-born star, and his bandmates eventually hit the road to perform mini gigs at schools up and down the country, Jay enjoyed every single minute. He was finally doing what he had set out to do, and doing it with four other fellas that he genuinely got on with. But even though they were well received by the kids in their classrooms, Jay was stunned when some were cheeky enough to shout out some rather naughty comments. 'At one of our schools we did an intro, during which we always said our names, and I was like, "Yeah! I'm Jay!" and I waited for a cheer. Before the cheer happened, this tiny little lad went, "Jay the Gay!" I was gutted.' But brave soldier that he is, Jay didn't take the silly comment to heart and carried on regardless, entertaining the kids as best as he could.

Probably the biggest highlight of this nationwide tour was stopping off at his old school, All Saints Catholic School. Walking back into the classroom was odd for him, as several years had past, and new pupils had taken his place. It was also weird for him to comprehend that the very same teachers who once used to tell him off and give him detention for being too chatty in class or for not doing his homework, were now talking to him as a grown-up and no longer a school kid.

Jay was especially pleased to be playing a gig at the school that morning, as some of his old school friends, such as Ewan Tomeny, David Hobbs, Catherine Kearney, and Megan Smith, had come along to offer him their support and catch up with what he'd been doing down in London for the past few months.

'It's great that we have been able to get here and it was great to see my friends in the audience supporting me,' he proudly said, after performing a handful of tracks in front of a crowd of 200 in the school gym. His mate Catherine also admitted how amazed she was by the band's performance and couldn't believe that it was her old school friend that she was watching gyrate up on stage.

'He looked excited that we were all there to

support him and you could just see that he was really touched that we were all there,' she said. Even though his mates predicted that his career was about to take off, and that he would end up living the pop star lifestyle that he had always dreamed of, they all said that although he would now be known as Jay from The Wanted, he was still the old James to them.

Also watching Jay sing and dance his heart out on that sunny morning were his cousins, Faye Riley and Evelyn Munton. Mesmerised by the group's tight routines and catchy singalong tunes, they said that while they and their family always believed that Jay would make it as a dancer one day, they couldn't believe that their flesh and blood was actually being chased around by screaming girls like the pop stars they had seen on the TV. Neither did they think that Jay really understood just how much his life was about to change. 'I don't think it's actually hit him yet as he's too calm about it all,' Faye told the local newspaper at the time.

Meanwhile, Jay's arguably toughest critic, Assistant Head Mistress Chris Young, could only find nice things to say about her former pupil. 'When he first came to the school James was really talented and it's lovely to see them all be so successful,' she said. 'James deserves it all. He was an excellent pupil and I am so proud and I wish them all the success in the world.'

With such praise heaped on him and possibilities for the band opening up all the time, such as an upcoming album and a potential tour, Jay admits that he can't wait to see what else could be waiting for him and his bandmates around the corner: 'I am really looking forward to what the future has in store.'

Getting to know... Max George

Age: 22

Date Of Birth: 06/09/1988

Hometown: Manchester

Star Sign: Virgo

Favourite Food: Dominos, full English, steak (as rare as it can be!)

Height: 5'8"

Eye Colour: Grey

Hair Colour: Dark Brown

Favourite Band: Queen

Football Team: Man City

Favourite Animal: Great White Shark

Favourite TV Show as a kid: *The Turtles*

Recent TV Show: *The X Factor*

Favourite Trainers: Nike

Status: Recently spotted snogging Vanessa White from The Saturdays

Dream Woman: Sinitta

Random Fact: Used to be on Man City's books.

Max George never wanted to be a pop star; Well, not to start with any way! No sooner could he walk then the cutesome little fella was demonstrating the kind of fancy footwork that his future bandmate Jay McGuiness could have done with to avoid being picked on in school. Football was a major talking point in the George household in Swinton, Manchester. His dad loved it, his granddad loved it, so it wasn't long before it was ingrained into the little lad that football was something of a religion to the family. And Manchester City football ground was their church.

As he grew up, the team became so important to him that all he wanted to do was to play for them. Pretty much all of his time was spent thinking about football, often his mind drifting off in class at school dreaming about the day he'd be there, scoring the winning goal against Manchester United, or helping England triumph at the World Cup. To ensure that his dreams would eventually come true, Max worked himself hard, kicking a ball around and honing his skills as much as he could.

Amazingly, his dedication and devotion to the sport and to his favourite football team eventually paid off, when he was spotted by the club bosses and asked to join their apprentice team. The suits at Manchester City could see that Max had what it took to go all the way, and gave him the opportunity to develop his skills even more under their watchful gaze. It all looked very promising for Max indeed.

After all that dreaming about joining his favourite team, he had achieved what he had set out to do, and he was convinced that the rest of his life was pretty much mapped out for him: he'd make it into the main team, play the field with the women, maybe even hook up with a pop star girlfriend like David Beckham and Ashley Cole had done and marry her.

With his head in the clouds and all these thoughts and plans swirling around in his mind, Max couldn't have predicted what was waiting for him around the corner and that it would change his future forever. During a game of footie, the young ace snapped his hip flexor – the muscle that joins the groin to the hip. Seeking immediate medical advice, he was devastated to discover that the injury meant that his footballing days were pretty much over, as he would have to spend weeks recovering, taking him away from vital training and it would affect his movement on the pitch long-term.

Coming to terms with the fact that a career in football was probably no longer an option for him, he decided that he'd try the next best thing – becoming a pop star. And having been told that he was a pretty good-looking fella and that he had a great singing voice, he reckoned he was on to a sure thing and took the brave step to audition for *The X Factor*, just so he could see if he actually did have what it took to make it big.

But was he really willing to put himself through the terror of having to face the ever-truthful Simon Cowell and possibly be ridiculed on the spot? Sure, his family and friends had told him time and time again that he had the looks and the voice to become a pop star, but what did they know? What if the Cowell didn't agree? He'd be utterly crushed. But deep down he knew he had to find out the truth, just to see if he really could make it, and reckoned it was better to find out how good he really was from the mouth of the most important person in the music industry today.

Nervously he headed off to the auditions, sailed through the preliminary round where candidates meet the show's producers, and then sang his heart out to Simon Cowell, Sharon Osborne and Louis Walsh. When he ended his audition, he nervously waited for their critique. And when it came, Max totally couldn't believe his ears when the fearsome Simon told him that he actually reminded him of a young Robbie Williams – only with a better voice! As the words tripped off Cowell's tongue, Max could feel himself burn with excitement. This had gone better than he thought! And when he was told they thought he was good enough to go on to the Boot Camp stage of the show, he was ready to explode.

Overjoyed, Max left the audition totally convinced that he was a potential pop star and felt more confident than ever that he had the talent to make it in the music industry, and be as successful as perhaps Robbie or

Take That! But sadly, things didn't quite work out the way he'd wanted it to. When Boot Camp time came around, Max suffered from a crisis of confidence and mucked up, failing to proceed any further in the competition. Years later, he admitted that his head just wasn't in it at the time.

Even though he was disappointed by his failure at *The X Factor*, Max continued to pursue his pop dreams. He thought he might be more successful as a member of a boyband, and he heard one was seeking members. He reckoned that working with a bunch of other boys would be a lot more fruitful for him. And he was right; he was snapped up as one fifth of the boyband Avenue, alongside four other fit lads called Ross Candy, Scott Clarke, Jonny Lloyd and Jamie Tinkler, who, like Max, had had previous music industry experience when he had made the final 50 of *Pop Idol 2* and tried but failed to represent the UK at *Eurovision*.

For the first few weeks, the band spent time getting to know each other, starting work on songs and working out how their voices blended together best.

But instead of gigging around the country like most up-and-coming bands do, their management team decided that the best way to give the boys as much as exposure as possible and the perfect foot in the door would be to have them appear on *The X Factor*.

Five months after they came together, the boys rocked up to the Manchester auditions, raring to go and brimming with confidence. No sooner had they stepped into the queue then producers from the TV company picked them out of the crowd to talk to the show's host, Kate Thornton. Excited to have been chosen to appear on the show, the boys told her that they were quietly confident that they could make it through to the Boot Camp round and maybe even all the way.

All the signs looked good when the boys bypassed the first round to face Simon, Sharon and Louis. Walking in with bravado, the boys showed the tough judges little nerves. As they did their introductions, Max was surprised that the judges didn't remember him from his previous time on the show. But Max didn't have time to worry about that, as the boys were asked to launch into their song, which was a harmonious version of Will Young's 'Leave Right now'. Once they'd finished, the boys looked at each other, pleased with their solid performance. They looked at the judges, expecting Simon, Sharon and Louis to be ecstatic to have stumbled across the newest, most fantastic boyband they had ever seen. But they were about to be disappointed. Simon told them that he thought their performance was only 'okay' and that he just 'didn't get it' to which a desperate Max pleaded that as they hadn't been together long, they had room to improve. But Simon still remained unconvinced, and told them that he wasn't going to put them through to Boot Camp. They were gutted. Even though there were three judges, it was always Simon's comments that meant the most! Nevertheless, Louis and Sharon obviously saw something in the five eager boys that Simon hadn't and gave them passes through to the next round.

Boot Camp proved be a little more successful for the Avenue boys, when their performance of 'To Love Somebody' guaranteed them a place in the Judges'

Homes round. It was here that the group faced their biggest competition yet, this time in the form of boyband Eton Road, a bunch of well scrubbed lads from Liverpool.

During this round, both bands put their hearts and souls into their performances, which left Louis facing a rather tricky dilemma. As far as he was concerned, both boybands sounded and looked great, which made it harder for him to choose between the two. Eventually, after much thought, the famed manager who turned Westlife and Boyzone into superstars, went with his gut instinct and chose Avenue, who literally jumped for joy with his decision. The boys couldn't believe that they were going through to the live shows. They could almost smell victory.

But sadly, Max was dealt another mighty blow, when their joy swiftly turned to despair after it was revealed in the press that Avenue were already signed up to a management agency, which was against the show rules. Louis was left in a predicament about what to do. Should he keep the boys on the show, knowing that they'd be massive successes on the live shows? Or would he have to abide by the show's rules and disqualify them?

Calling the boys to his office, Louis told them that he had made a decision. 'I have thought long and hard and this has been one of the hardest decisions I've ever had to make,' he said to them. 'You broke the rules and you stopped somebody else getting into the competition, the decision has been made – you are disqualified from the competition. You lied to me.'

The boys were shattered by the news. Tough boy Max couldn't contain his emotions and broke down in tears. He was crushed that after having been given a massive opportunity, it had been cruelly snatched away from them again.

'I was devastated,' he recalled years later. 'Being from Manchester, I grew up with Take That mania. I wanted the same, and thought it might happen, and then it was taken away from me.' However, the years that passed helped Max get over the utter devastation he felt. 'I loved every minute of *The X Factor*,' he said, 'because growing up, I always used to watch *Pop Idol* and all those shows – I'm sure most kids did. I look back on it and I have nothing but brilliant memories of *The X Factor* – apart from being disqualified, which was hard to take, because we'd got there and then had it taken away from us. But saying that, if that hadn't happened, I wouldn't be here with these lads.'

In spite of the public humiliation of being disqualified from *The X Factor*, it appeared that there was still life in Avenue yet. So following a member reshuffle which saw the departure of Jamie Tinkler, due to 'musical differences' and the introduction of newboy Andy Brown, the band were relaunched at a spectacular launch party in London. It was thanks, in part, to Max's dad, who had taken the boys on board after *The X Factor* debacle and 'knocked down doors at the labels' and got them signed. Their first single, 'Last Goodbye', was a perky pop stomper but sadly failed to prick up the ears of the record buying public, and failed to light up the charts. This flop swiftly put an end to Avenue, and the band went their separate ways.

But the stars were shining down on Max. In the

summer of 2009 he was approached to audition for a new boyband – The Wanted. And the rest, as they say, is history.

This time round Max brought with him the experience of Avenue. 'This time I've learned to put more on myself than be told what to do by people. It's good to have your own involvement, get your views across and your opinions, because at least if you have your own opinions, they don't have to listen but at least you've put it forward. Even when we didn't want something in Avenue we didn't speak up. We write our own songs in this group and we didn't do that before.'

Getting to know...
Nathan Sykes

Age: 17

Date Of Birth: 18/04/93

Hometown: Gloucester

Star Sign: Aries

Favourite Food: Spag Bol, Chinese, Soup, Roast dinners

Height: 5ft 9ish

Eye Colour: Green/Blue

Hair Colour: Brown

Favourite Band: Boyz II Men

Football Team: Manchester United

Favourite Animal: Cat

Favourite TV Show as a kid: *Saturday Show (BBC)*

Recent TV Show: *Match of the Day!/Britain's Got Talent*

Favourite Trainers: Converse

Status: Single

Dream Woman: Kate Thornton

Random Fact: He's the tidiest member of The Wanted

There was never any doubt that Nathan Sykes would one day make it in to the world of showbiz. No sooner was he born than he was demonstrating to his businessman dad, Harry and music teacher mum, Karen just what a powerful set of lungs he had. Once he could speak, he treated his family and friends to impromptu singing performances whenever he got the chance. Music became an obsession for the young boybander-in-the-making, and he took part in any productions that came along at Longlevens Junior School. At seven, he started to learn the piano, though now admits that he wasn't as good as he had hoped. 'I've got to say I was absolutely shocking. My little sister was much better than me.'

By the time he was nine, Nathan was making some very serious inroads to the world of celebrity. First, he took part in a TV singing competition called *Britney's Karaoke Kriminals*, in which he showed off a most powerful voice for a boy so weeny. Appearing on the show was a great learning experience for the wannabe star, and gave him a great insight into what he would have to get used to years down the line when he made it in to The Wanted.

Even though he was a little nervous up on stage, in front of an audience, in a studio with big lights and surrounded by camera crews and production staff, he still managed to keep calm. In fact, once he started singing and saw the reaction of people around him, he realized that this was just what he wanted from life. He loved the buzz of being on stage and singing – he knew he wanted this feeling to last forever.

Winning the competition gave him a massive burst of excitement. It was all well and good receiving a massive round of applause at the end of the song, but to be considered to have had the best performance in the whole competition was just the icing on the cake. What made the experience even more exciting, was that he received not only a trophy but a skirt that Britney Spears herself wore in the film *Crossroads*.

But the Britney competition wasn't his only chance to appear on TV. He also took part in a mock version of *The X Factor* on ITV's *Ministry Of Mayhem*. Once again, the buzz of performing in the studio made him want to make this his life.

But Nathan's talent didn't stop at just singing. Whilst he indeed had an amazing voice, he was also a pretty nifty mover on the dance floor, and entered several dance competitions, including the Dance 2002 competition at Montel's nightclub in Tewkesbury. This saw the lithe fella prancing about the stage in a black leather cap and fingerless gloves – something Nathan probably wouldn't be caught dead wearing these days.

With his heart set on a career in singing and dancing, Nathan asked his parents if instead of attending the local secondary school, The Crypt School, he could attend the prestigious Sylvia Young Theatre School in London that helped train the likes of Billie Piper, Spice Girl Emma Bunton to name just two. His parents, who could see that their son was gifted, wholeheartedly agreed and arranged an interview with the school. Unsurprisingly, Nathan impressed the panel so much that they offered him the Emma Priest scholarship for musical theatre. Because he was so young, his parents decided that he would continue to live with them in Gloucester, and that he

The WANTED

The boys hang out backstage at the Transformation Trust 1st Birthday Party - London

SIVA

JAY

NATHAN

TOM

MAX

Max

Nathan

Tom

Siva

Jay

would commute to London daily. The journey was long – three hours each way – but Nathan didn't mind in the slightest, because it meant that he got to do what he loved most – singing and dancing. However, Nathan admits that his schoolmates thought he was mental for the doing his daily trek: 'They used to think "here comes the nutter that gets up at 5 every morning."'

Though he must have been tired from his busy week, Nathan still found time to perform back in his home town. He not only appeared in the regional finals of the Live and Unsigned competition in 2008; he also won the Undiscovered Youth Talent Competition at a Christian Youth Project called The Door with his performance of 'Mack the Knife'. Brendan Conboy, the manager of The Door and organiser of the competition, says he is thrilled that the boy he discovered has achieved so much success with The Wanted. 'The first time I ever saw Nathan perform was at the Oakridge fête when he was about 13. He works so hard, and he deserves to be where he is now. What I love about Nathan is he's still kept his feet on the ground. I'm still in touch with him through Facebook and it's good to see how he's getting on.'

When he finished his studies at Sylvia Young, Nathan returned to Ribston Hall High School to study for his A Levels at sixth form, but not before he had auditioned for a new boyband. As he began his term, he was delighted to discover that his audition had been successful and that he had made it into the final five boys for The Wanted. This put Nathan in a dilemma – what should he do? Should he stick with his studies or should he quit school and try his luck with the band? 'Obviously you never know what is going to happen. Singing is my dream but I need something to fall back on,' he wisely said, just as the band was first starting out. 'I'm going to take my exams seriously. You can't take these things for granted.'

To start with, Nathan reckoned he would be able to live in London and carry on his studies without any problems. Even though he had moved to London to live with the rest of the band, he continued to go back to school whenever he could. 'It was honestly very weird going into school then. I knew I was in the band already but I couldn't really tell anyone,' Nathan recalls. 'So when the careers adviser asked me what I was going to be, I was going, "Pop singer!" But I worked hard.'

But as his touring schedule became tougher and busier, he made a drastic decision - that he would put his studies on hold for the time being. When he told his teachers about his decision he was pleased to discover that they were very supportive and told him that he would be able to come back anytime he wanted to finish off his A-Levels.

His decision was also supported by his parents, who understood that The Wanted was an opportunity that he simply couldn't turn down. 'From my point of view, Nathan has worked tirelessly to achieve this goal ever since the age of six,' his dad Harry said. 'He has been wowing crowds for years, and now he's performing to hundreds of thousands of people.'

But while his dad was ecstatic that his boy Nathan had made it into the band, there was one person in his life who wasn't as easily impressed – his 13-year old sister, who reckoned being in a boyband was a bit uncool. 'When I first went home and told Jess I was in a boyband she thought it was quite funny,' Nathan said, just after 'All Time Low' hit the top spot on the charts. 'She said I had no street cred because I was in a 'boyband' but I think she has been convinced now. She is really happy for me and I am hoping I have a bit of street cred back now.'

Making it into The Wanted meant that Nathan had to leave the comfort of his Gloucester home and move to London, where he would have to shack up with four total strangers in a house in south London. Luckily, any worries Nathan might have had about living with a bunch of guys he hadn't met before were cast aside, as the fellas all got on really well straightaway, with Nathan admitting that they 'fitted together like bits of a puzzle'.

Even though he was living away from home, Nathan made sure he kept in contact with his family back in Gloucester. 'I ring my mum and sister every day,' he said. 'My friends at home have been really supportive and whenever I have a few days off I always try to go home. I think mum is pretty proud, she is chuffed to bits and really supportive.'

Living away from Gloucester was pretty easy for Nathan. Even though he was the youngest of the boys, he felt like the grown-up, sensible one. 'I'm a bit of an old man,' he says. 'I just sit in the corner with my cup of tea and take it all in.' He even admitted that while the rest of guys hit the bars to enjoy a boozy night out, he always keeps a watchful eye over them, just incase they get into any scrapes. 'I have been their minder, watching on while they've been getting wasted over the past few weeks as I can't drink yet,' he revealed the week their debut single 'All Time Low' was released, adding, 'if we get to number one I'll be stuck drinking tea while the others go out partying. I'll just sit in the corner with my chocolate digestives.'

Nathan only has to wait until April 2011 when he turns eighteen, so that he can finally join his new mates, living it up in swanky bars and clubs instead of merely performing at them. But for now, Nathan is just happy in the knowledge that he and the band have been hugely successful and that his dreams of pop superstardom and having a number one single have come true.

'I always wanted to do singing as a career even though people would tell me it was really difficult to get into,' he says. 'But I was prepared to put in a lot of hard work to do what I wanted. I hoped I would be number one when I was younger but I never thought it would actually happen.'

It just goes to show – if you put your mind to something, your dreams might just come true.

Getting to know...
Siva Kaneswaran

Age: 21

Date Of Birth: 16/11/1988

Hometown: Dublin, Ireland

Star Sign: Scorpio

Favourite Food: Shepherd's pie, Brownies, Stew

Height: 6ft 1

Eye Colour: Brown

Hair Colour: Black with a few ginger hairs

Favourite Band: Switchfoot

Football Team: Manchester City or Bolton

Favourite Animal: Dog

Favourite TV Show as a Kid: *Buffy the Vampire Slayer*

Recent TV Show: *Family Guy*

Favourite Trainers: Y3 Yoji Yamamoto for Adidas

Status: Has a long-term girlfriend

Dream Woman: Beyoncé

Random Fact: Siva is one of eight siblings

With his dashing, good looks, high cheek bones and chiselled jaw, it was inevitable that Siva Kaneswaran would be famous in some way. However, growing up in the notorious Corduff area of Blanchardstown, near Dublin, Ireland, it seemed for a while that the search for fame might be a tough one. But Siva and his twin brother Kumar were lucky to have been born into a family destined to hit the big time, as they had two sisters and two other brothers who had already tasted fame to look up to, as they strived to make it big.

Perhaps the family's success in showbiz was to do with the fact that the eight siblings were blessed with stunning good looks, which were passed onto them by their equally striking window cleaner father. Hailing from Singapore, Kaneswaran Sr was a very popular figure in the family's local area, and it was he who passed on to his children the love of music.

The first of the siblings to launch a music career was the second eldest child, Hazel, who fronted a little known band called Dove. However, it was her appearance on the TV show, *Popstars The Rivals* that really put Hazel in the spotlight. The then 22 year old wannabe was so desperate to get into what would eventually become Girls Aloud, that she auditioned whilst being eight months pregnant. This fact troubled the judges: after all, if she made it through to the live shows, would she end up having her baby on stage? However, her vocals proved to be so great that they decided she was worth taking a risk on and selected her as one of the ten girls who might make the final line up of Girls Aloud.

But her dreams were cruelly shattered: when as she was about to move into the *Popstars* house, it emerged that she was actually ten days too old to take part in the show. She was told that she would have to be disqualified from the competition, which subsequently left a gap in the band for a certain Kimberley Walsh to join Cheryl Cole, Sarah Harding and Nadine Coyle in the final stages of the series. Despite this setback, Hazel dusted herself and went on to carve out a successful music and TV career in Ireland and was even a judge on Ireland's most popular talent show *You're A Star!*

But Hazel wasn't the only Kaneswaran who had stars in their eyes. Siva's older brother David also had dreams of pop superstardom and tried his luck in a boyband called Zoo.

While the band never really made it in the UK, the five piece were moderately successful in their home country and had hits with 'Poison', 'Pour Some Sugar On Me' and even recorded a song ironically called 'Wanted'. Sadly for David, the band didn't last and he eventually moved behind the scenes to focus on songwriting and producing.

Siva's other older brother Trevor also attempted to break into music, taking part in *The X Factor* in 2008. His dashing looks and amazing voice helped him through to the Boot Camp stages, but sadly he never made it any further. Trevor's family still reckon he has what it takes to make it in the biz. 'We used to slag him saying he learned to sing before he could talk, as he has been at it since he was three years old, when he went in for this local talent show and he won it. It's all he has ever wanted to do,' sister Gail recalls. 'He really wants to make it big, and who wouldn't want to be in a programme like *X Factor*? Ever since Hazel was in *Popstars*, our whole family has been mad about the show and we always watch it.'

But despite his *X Factor* disappointment Trevor is still very much into music and is busy writing and recording, so don't be surprised if you see yet another Kaneswaran hitting the charts in the near future.

With most of the older members of the family trying their hand at the fame game, it was inevitable that Siva would want to follow in their footsteps. But before he even thought about being a singer, Siva and his twin Kumar decided to try modelling instead, just like their eldest sister Gail, who had been a successful model for years. With their exotic features and perfect bone structure the two boys easily landed themselves loads of modelling assignments, and went on to appear in style mags and adverts.

But after a while, Siva grew a little of bored of posing and catwalk shows and, having learnt how to play the guitar at fifteen, decided that it was a music career he wanted to pursue instead. Sister Hazel was thrilled and with all her musical contacts, was instrumental in setting him on the right path. But Hazel was more than just a big sister to Siva and his brother Kumar. She was more like a parent. When their father died of a heart attack in 2005, when Siva was just sixteen, she and older sister Gail pretty much took his place in looking after the family with their mother, Lily. That meant encouraging them to reach for the skies and try to attain their dreams. So Siva did just that.

One of his first breaks came when he and Kumar landed the roles of two twin brothers in a boyband called Fade Up, in the shortlived ITV drama *Rock Rivals*, which starred Michelle Collins. The show was like a dramatized version of *The X Factor*, with a bunch of contestants battling it out to the fictional reality show.

Although Siva and Kumar had very few lines in the show, it was a great platform for the boys and gave them the much needed experience of working in front of cameras. It also gave Siva his first taste of what it was like to be a member of a boyband, albeit a fictional one.

Although it was Siva's first big job, he apparently settled into the show easily and proved a popular cast member. Sadly, the show wasn't exactly a smash hit, but that didn't get Siva down. On the contrary, it merely fed his hunger for success. After this, he wanted more and so he kept his ear to the ground for any opportunities that might arise.

And it wasn't long before someone suggested that he and his brother try their luck in *The X Factor*. After a little deliberation, where they weighed up the pros and cons of appearing on a reality show as big as that, the two boys eventually decided to give it a miss: 'It just wasn't for me,' Siva explained. 'I'd rather go the step-by-step route rather than do something too fast.'

And then, as if by magic, along came The Wanted, straight out of the blue. Unlike the other boys, who had auditioned for a place in the band, the team putting The Wanted together came across a picture of Siva and Kumar and approached their modelling agency to find out if they could sing. When they were told that they were more than just pretty faces, they enthusiastically asked them to come and try out for the group. The result? Siva was in but Kumar didn't make the grade. 'I felt a bit bad as my twin brother didn't get in,' he recalls. 'But he's chuffed for me though and there are no hard feelings.'

For Siva, joining a boyband was tough, as he was the only member of the band to have a girlfriend. 'Her name is Nareesha and we met a long time ago in Belfast. She's a shoe designer and comes from Jay's home town of Nottingham! So we've had to get used to each other's accents. She's living down the road from me, very close.'

But Siva has admitted that that when he first joined the band and began their extensive touring around the country, he and Nareesha suffered a few teething problems, due to the fact that he was never around to spend some quality time with her. 'It was quite difficult for us to start with, but I think she realizes that I have to put a lot of time into the band. It was only the two of us at the beginning - now it's seven of us!' Their relationship has also been tested a few times following dubious press speculation about Siva. According to some reports, Siva had supposedly been spotted flirting with Vanessa from The Saturdays. But this particular story was rubbished straightaway by Vanessa herself, who went on record to say the pair of them were just good friends who had got to know each on the road. And bearing in mind that The Saturdays and The Wanted were managed by the same team, it was pretty inevitable that the bands would forge friendships along the line.

Then there was the story about Rihanna meeting Siva in a club, asking for his number, and sending him loads of texts. Amazingly, the story was partly true, in that they did indeed meet. 'I was in Mahiki and then suddenly Rihanna came up to me and started chatting away,' he revealed. 'I was cool with it, she's very tall. I had my girlfriend with me so I had to cut the conversation short. In the end we went to Greggs for a bacon and cheese melt.'

But Siva says that Nareesha doesn't have to worry and is glad that she understands that fabricated stories will hit the papers from time to time, and that she shouldn't always believe what she reads. Siva says he can't wait to spend some time with her when the band's promotions come to an end. 'We'll get a bit of a break soon, maybe just one interview a day instead of seven. We don't mind the work but we'll need our holidays.' But hardworking Siva understands that to maintain the band's evergrowing fanbase and to continue their amazing success, he and the boys have to put the hard work in. And that will mean working away from home and loved ones.

'All that travelling and late nights paid off when we released our single, because all those people who saw us added up and the single sky-rocketed,' he says, adding, 'The attention from the paparazzi and everyone has gone crazy. Everybody wants a bit of you.'

If he needed any more inspiration to take his new job as seriously as possible, then he only has to look at his old friend from Dublin, and one fifth of the Saturdays, Una Healy, to prove that honing your talents, working hard and having a lot of determination can open a lot of doors.

'I used to listen to her songs on My Space all the time because I listened to all kinds of music,' Siva says. 'I was only a kid when I first met her as Una knows my sisters, because when you're on the Dublin scene everyone knows you as it's really only a village. Now we're good friends and I'm chuffed for her and everyone in The Saturdays because they really deserve to be number one.'

Getting to know...
Tom Parker

Age: 22

Date Of Birth: 04/08/1988

Hometown: Bolton

Star Sign: Leo

Favourite Food: Indian, Italian

Height: 5ft 10

Eye Colour: Hazel

Hair Colour: Brown

Favourite Band: Oasis

Football Team: Bolton Wanderers

Favourite Animal: Parrot

Favourite TV Show as a Kid: *Rosie and Jim*

Recent TV Show: *The Inbetweeners*

Favourite Trainers: Reebok

Status: Single

Dream Woman: Kate Thornton

Random Fact: He's the tidiest member of The Wanted

Gorgeous Tom Parker had never really considered a career in the music industry. He had never been a kid who had lay awake at night dreaming of being famous or being a pop star. In fact, he spent most of his early years being rather clumsy, and he has a bunch of scars to prove it. Look closely and you will see that he has one on his nose; which he got after picking off a chicken pox scab, and another one on his forehead; which he got after he ran through a patio door, thinking it was open. He also has a scar above his eyebrow; which he gained after falling off a rocking horse, and one on his cheek which he sustained during a rather vigorous football match!

But all that changed when, at 16, he picked up the guitar for the first time and discovered that he had found a new direction in his life.

'My guitar pretty much changed my life,' the husky voiced joker of The Wanted has said. 'I was never really into music. Now it's like my best friend, wherever I am I just pick it up and start playing.' Fortunately for him, he also discovered that he had a pretty good voice – somewhere between Liam Gallagher and Kelly Jones from The Stereophonics

– although he admits that as with the guitar he has trained himself. 'I've got a really throaty, rock voice, I'm glad I never had any singing lessons, they try to teach you a certain way. I just kinda taught myself.'

Now knowing what he wanted to do, Tom set about trying to get jobs in the industry. One of his early attempts was as Mark Owen in a Take That tribute band. This job gave him his first opportunity to perform in front of crowds of people. Up on stage, he totally loved the buzz he got from hearing people singing along to the songs. But what frustrated him most, was that the audience were singing along to Take That songs, while what he really wanted was to have them singing along to his songs instead!

His next step was to try his luck on *The X Factor*, just as Max had done before him. But unlike his future bandmate, poor Tom didn't even make it past the first stage of the competition, which meant he never got to see the judges. 'A producer told me that I wasn't going any further,' he recalled. Feeling dejected, Tom, who at the time was unemployed and claiming jobseeker's allowance, stumbled across an advert in The Stage seeking boys for a new band.

At first he wasn't sure if he could face the same kind of rejection he had experienced at *The X Factor,* and considered not bothering to apply. But then he thought to himself; what did he have to lose? 'I just thought I might as well go for it,' he said. 'My confidence was really knocked after I went on *X Factor*. I was trying out for a solo career but looking back I was not great and I do believe it was for the best.' So he auditioned, and crossed his fingers that perhaps this time might be his lucky break, but the poor fella had to wait some nine months until he discovered that he had been successful, and had landed himself a place in the band! He couldn't believe that after being knocked back from *The X Factor* he was now in a proper band. And so, once again, his confidence was restored and he threw himself into the job. He was amazed by the response the band got when they finally hit the road. 'It's unbelievable. We're not your typical boyband. We love a drink, chase women and break the rules. People will hopefully see we're just five ordinary lads having fun.'

Coming Together

Imagine how it feels when you start school for the first time: nerves build in your tummy as you worry about what kind of people you are going to be stuck with for the next few years. So imagine what it must have been like for The Wanted boys when they met for the first time, knowing that these were the guys they would not only be working with, but living with at the same time. That meant that twenty four seven, they would be eating, sleeping and singing together.

Luckily, when they met they all got on like a house on fire, but Max remembers that the initial meeting was tough. 'It's one of those times when you try and make more jokes than you normally would. I'm sweating now at the thought of it. But we got on pretty quick, to be fair.'

Jay jokes that when he first laid eyes on striking Siva, he wanted to leave the band, fearing there was just no way he would be able to compete with him in the looks department.

But Jay needn't have worried about being hidden in Siva's beautiful shadow, as all five guys have developed their own very different sets of fans since hitting the big time. 'We're all very different so hopefully people will like one of us! I'm really into my football and am a bit cheeky,' Max says. 'Siva's pretty laidback and really zen, Jay's a bit of an indie-kid and then Nathan – you think he's all young and cute but actually he's really dead dry and sarcastic. Oh yeah, and Tom – he's just a lad from Bolton.'

After their initial meeting, the boys moved into a house in south London and proceeded to turn it into a bachelor pad, complete with table football, a dart board and computer games, not to mention a fridge stocked full of beer and a freezer stacked with pizzas. 'It's a lad's flat,' Max boasts. 'No girls allowed.'

Boys will be boys, and if you were to pop around to see them, don't be surprised if the place looks like a tip. Why? Because the boys just can't keep the place tidy, and don't even bother about asking them for a clean cup or plate, they wouldn't know where to find one. All five will admit that they are not the most house proud guys you could meet, Tom is, the rest of the band agree, the messiest, and 'breeds filth', or so Jay would have us believe. So to ensure that the house wasn't overrun with giant rats, the record company arranged for a little home help to pop by regularly. 'We have a cleaner who comes in twice a week! She's a machine, she ploughs through the whole house. She even does our washing and ironing.' Lucky boys! What would they do without her?

When they aren't busy working or touring around the country, their London home is their base where they can find solitude away from work and the flashing paparazzi. But sometimes, when the mood takes them, they might head out to a local pub for a few drinks, led by Tom and Max.

'We pretty much leather it at any party going,' Tom says. 'But all the lads know how to have a laugh – maybe Nath's not reached that crazy part of his life yet, but we'll bring it out in him soon enough!'

If they don't fancy going out the boys prefer to stay home, slobbing out on their beds, reading books and magazines, playing computer games or watching sport or films on Sky in Max's room.

It's when they're lazing about like this that their icky bad habits come to the fore.

For example, Tom, according to Nathan, has a nasty habit of breaking wind and 'wafting it about' when he's proud of it. Meanwhile, Jay horrifies his housemates by cutting his toenails in front of everyone with the kitchen scissors. ('They ping every where,' he says shamelessly.) Even gorgeous Siva has a dodgy habit – 'I pick my nose a bit' – which he even reckons is 'quite manky'. Yes, Siva, it is!

When they're not upsetting each other with their antisocial behaviour, the boys like to keep their gorgeous bodies in trim by working out as much as they can, especially if they have a photo or video shoot coming up. You can normally find Max toning his muscles with his dumbbells in his room – usually topless – and Tom doing press-ups in the stairwell. 'Dedication,' Tom wisely says, 'gets you places.'

And on the subject of looking fine, it would appear that all five boys are pretty fussy about the way they look, and all take their time making sure that they look as hot as can be.

'I can be a bit obsessed about how I look,' Tom

admits. 'It's my hair. I'm forever looking at it in the mirror. Nathan also isn't ashamed to say that it takes time to create perfection. 'I quite openly admit that I take the longest to get ready, but I end up looking the worst. Being slow is probably my worst habit.'

Who cares how long they take to look good – just as long as they look as great as they normally do. Right?

The road to success

When 'All Time Low' smashed into the number one spot, it came as something of a surprise: The Wanted seemed to have burst out of nowhere. But the truth is, the boys had been working very hard for months, travelling all around the country and performing to thousands of kids at schools and clubs.

Despite the fact that the boys were raring to go and strut their stuff, they surprisingly found the build-up to their first performance a nerve wracking experience. Waking up at 4am on the morning of the gig, Siva groggily admitted that he had been suffering from butterflies the night before, nervous about performing in front of an audience for the first time, and admitted that he was worried that he wouldn't be able to breathe when he got to the school. Meanwhile, Max, who normally is the ever confident member of The Wanted, confessed that he wasn't feeling all that well. 'I feel awful,' he admitted in the tour van. 'My throat is awful. Look at the extremes I have to go to – I am eating porridge with honey in.'

However, when they got to the school, the fellas seemed to be a lot more relaxed and prepared for the show by wasting time larking about in the headmaster's office, playing table tennis across his desk. Even Max started to relax and was able to ease the tension with a couple of dodgy gags, such as, 'What did the grape say when I stood on it. Not much, it just let out a little wine.' (Note to Max – don't give up the day job!)

Initial reactions to the band were, the boys will readily admit, a little lukewarm, probably because no one really knew who they were. But as they travelled from one to school to the next, and as fans began talking about them online and reading about them in magazines, the kids became more and more excited whenever the boys dropped by. Some were so enthusiastic about their visit that on occasions they actually stormed the stage to get even closer to the boys!

As time went on and the fans became even more over zealous, the boys discovered just how forward some of them could be. 'I had my bum pinched about ten times,' Max said of one school visit. 'And one of them had a right grab, and clung onto it for ages!' Siva's perfect tush also proved popular with the girls. 'I've had a few bum grabs outside Capital Radio - and they took pictures of the bum grabs, and put them on Twitter.'

But the boys realize that a few posterior pinches now and again are hazards of the job that they will have to get used to. 'You have to enjoy all that, don't you?' he reasoned. 'You can't go, "That's rubbish!" It can get a bit weird sometimes, and then you have to check yourself. We've been grabbed everywhere you can imagine.'

Of course, there is a plus side for the boys, in that many of their fans are rather attractive, which makes the single lads in the band very happy indeed! But despite feeling like kids in a candy shop, they have to be careful when it comes to mixing business with pleasure.

'Some are pretty attractive so we have to grit our teeth and resist temptation but I'm sure at some point it will happen,' Max says. 'But if we're performing live, me and Tom give each other the eye. We're like

"4 o'clock", over there. Look at the cogs on that!'

The boys have even admitted that they would actually date a fan, but only depending on how they presented themselves to them. 'How they come and introduce themselves is the key,' Jay says. 'If they come up to you and scream, then you're in the mindset of 'do the autograph', but if someone comes up and introduces themselves, and says they like the band, or even if they say they hate the band, it's just a chat, then it's a different ball game.'

Randy Tom also reckons that he could be tempted into dating a fan, even though he says he can understand why most pop stars tend to go on dates with people in the same line of work. 'All the celebrities try to keep their relationships in the music industry,' he says. 'and I understand why, cos it's hard to tell whether people like you for who you are. But if I meet the right person, then it wouldn't matter if they were a fan or not.'

But if you think the boys are lady magnets, think again. Just because the boys are gorgeous and successful chart-topping pop stars, it doesn't mean that they can have any girl they want. Take poor

Jay, for example. One evening he and the boys had gone to a club for some fun. During the night he spied a girl he thought was hot. Bravely, he tiptoed over to her and showed her that he was interested in her. Unfortunately for him, whatever lines he used and no matter how hard he tried to flirt, his efforts were fruitless and the girl pushed him away and disappeared into the night. Even more unfortunate for Jay, his rejection was keenly observed by Max and Tom, who found the incident absolutely hilarious. Well, don't worry Jay. There are plenty more fish in the sea!

All Time Low

From the very start of the song, with its edgy string opening and cool vocals, it was clear that 'All Time Low' was a song that once heard would never be forgotten. But songs don't just become hits overnight. To get the records in the chart, a lot of hard work has to go into promoting the record.

The boys have to work day and night, trying to get as many people to hear their single as possible. It's not as easy it as sounds. Just because a group releases a record, it doesn't mean people will go out and buy it. These days, with so many records battling to make it in the chart, it's important to get good radio airplay for the song. The most important station is Radio 1, which is hard to infiltrate. If they won't play the record, then it's harder to get it heard by the public, making it even harder to chart. To combat this, pop stars have to travel the country to appear on regional radio, the local stations situated in the parts of the country that are not normally visited by pop stars. And this is how The Wanted managed to build up an awareness about the record. Of course, it also helped that the boys were signed to a major label and that the PR looking after the band was the same team who represented the likes of Girls Aloud, The Saturdays, JLS and Cheryl Cole. This meant that it was far easier for The Wanted to get their foot in the door. If they hadn't had a great team of people behind them, they would have found it a lot harder to appear on radio shows.

As important as radio stations are in creating a buzz around a brand new act, TV is even better, due to the simple fact you can actually watch them do what they do best! So in the weeks leading up to the release of the single, the boys performed their songs on as many TV shows as they could get themselves on, appearing on shows such as *GMTV*, *T4* and *Big Brother's Little Brother*.

Of course, the boys can't be everywhere all of the time. Therefore, a pop promo for the single had to be made, which would be shown on music channels like *MTV*, *The Box* and *Smash Hits*. While the final product may have looked slick and ultra glamorous, with the boys looking sexy and brooding as coloured paint exploded around them, the reality was a totally different matter altogether.

The boys had to rock up to a cold warehouse on the outskirts of London at the crack of dawn and record their parts numerous times over the next twenty-four hours. On the morning of the shoot the boys were feeling a little nervous, as it was the first time they had filmed a video as a group. Before they were picked up by their tour manager, they did some last minute workouts in their rooms so that their muscles looked extra pumped on camera.

The shoot wasn't without its problems. During his solo shoot Jay lost his footing on the rubble and tumbled to the floor in front of the whole production crew. Once they were sure he wasn't hurt, everyone around him burst out laughing, as Jay is famed for his clumsiness. Luckily, he saw the funny side and reshot the scene again perfectly. Meanwhile, Max was left a touch embarrassed when the music playback suddenly stopped during filming and Max continued to sing. Normally that wouldn't have been too bad, but as he had been jokingly singing out of tune, he was left feeling a little silly indeed, worried that those who didn't know how talented he was would think that that was his true voice. 'It was just like when you get caught singing a really cheesy song in your car,' he said afterwards, blushing cutely.

When the video was complete the boys were impressed by what they saw, even though they giggled all the way through at the way they saw themselves on screen. But they were so proud that they had shot their first ever video, something they would cherish for the rest of their lives.

With the video being shown on the telly, and the single finally in the shops, the boys took to the road once again to do some record signings at music stores in cities around the country. If they had any fears that fans wouldn't come out to see them, they didn't have them for long as their queues for the signing stretched around the block. When the band performed at the Westfield shopping centre in London, they were shocked that 5,000 fans waited up to six hours to see them sing their hit. The press described the wild scenes as being reminiscent of Take That's early days

– though most of the girls who had turned up on the day with armfuls of gifts for the boys such as iPods, cuddly toys and underwear, were probably too young to remember Take That's beginnings.

The day before the boys found out how well 'All Time Low' had performed in the chart, they played a gig at London's Heaven club, where they sang exclusive songs from their album, plus a very special version of Cheryl Cole's 'Fight For This Love'. The crowd went wild and gave them a very warm reception, giving the boys even more of an indication about how well their single was going to do in the chart.

Next day, the boys gathered together around a radio so they could hear the countdown for themselves. As the DJ got closer and closer to the number one spot, the boys grew more and more excited about the prospect of achieving a chart topper with their very first single.

The boys had previously said that they would have been happy with a top 40 hit. But to have a number one with their first try would just be amazing. Especially for Max, who had never achieved anything like such a feat with his previous boyband, Avenue.

When 'All Time Low' was announced as the number one song, the boys went crazy and celebrated with champagne.

'We can't quite believe it!' Nathan said upon hearing the news. 'We were over the moon when we found out - and we're still buzzing from it now! The day before the single came out, we said we'd be happy for it just to make the top 40. None of us was sure which way it was going to go.'

The day after their chart position was announced the jubilant boys rocked up to London club Whiskey Mist to celebrate their success, where they met up with Leona Lewis, who Max had met during his time on *The X Factor*, and didn't roll home until after 6am. According to the papers the next day, the boys had a wild night, drinking so much alcohol that they could barely remember what had happened. One newspaper said that Siva was barely able to string a sentence together. Meanwhile, party animal Tom admitted that the lads were 'determined to get me bladdered as it was also my 22nd birthday this week. They did - but I got a snog so I'm happy.'

Max summed up the feelings of all the boys when

he said: 'It's been the most incredible week of our lives but we're all now feeling the effects of it!'

Nathan, who wasn't able to get tipsy as he's still too young to drink, sensibly said that while he was just as thrilled as the others about their amazing success, he was looking forward to their second single 'Heart Vacancy'. 'We're having such a good time but we have to keep up the good work,' he said. 'It won't be long before we're focusing on the next single, which is out in October.'

And what can fans expect from the new record? Well something very different, Nathan has revealed. 'It's a ballad,' he explains. 'But not your typical boyband ballad, because there's no big key-change-stand-up moment in it. It's just a big, catchy record that we're all really fond of and we hope everyone else likes it as much as we do!'

He also explained that the video, which was shot in Croatia, is a lot 'less frantic' than their first pop promo. A lot of people must have looked at the 'All Time Low' video and thought, 'Who the hell are these guys and why are they jumping around like idiots?' This one has a storyline and we each tell a part of it.

We had a lot of fun filming it.'

'It's stunningly shot,' Jay reveals. 'It's more like a movie. It's like a story with a cast, and we're kind of commenting on it. The girls in it are stunningly beautiful. It's not cheesy. We didn't want it to be cheesy.'

He also explained how welcome they were made to feel by the locals. 'While we were filming it, they were all coming out of their houses, and when we left, loads of them were crying! Word spread really fast that we were shooting a video, and there were all these girls between fourteen to eighteen, popping over to see us filming. When we finished, one of the girls came up to me, and she was bawling, crying. They'd only known us for about two hours. But these days we make girls cry wherever we go!'

And what of the rest of the album? Well, fans can look forward to the Robbie Williams-esque 'Let's Get Ugly', the dancetastic 'Lose My Heart' and 'Behind Bars'. However, Nathan says he has a current favourite that he can't wait for fans to get their ears around. 'There's a track called 'Golden' that I love to bits. It's like nothing else on the album as it's got quite an unusual sound. For that reason it probably won't be a single, but it's a great track for the album and shows a different side to us. It takes us far away from that typical boyband sound.'

The Album

While The Wanted don't mind being called a boyband, it is clear from their amazing songs that they are not your typical one. 'All Time Low', with its anthemic Kings Of Leon inspired melody, was a song that blew previous boyband tunes out of the water. And the fellas couldn't be happier about the great reaction it received, as from the outset, they were intent on making boybands cool again!

'You won't find us sitting on stools in our suits, and standing up for the key change!' Tom declared. During one rehearsal someone dared to suggest that they try some stools out during a routine, which the boys rejected out of hand. 'We were in a rehearsal and somebody brought some stools in, and we were like, "No, take them back!" Some people can pull off a suit, but we're not that bothered.'

In fact, the boys have no interest in following in the footsteps of balladeers like Westlife. They have their sights on bigger fish, and plan to share some of the success that their main rivals JLS are currently enjoying. 'Well, hopefully one day we'll be in that arena,' Jay said. 'But at the minute we're just trying to achieve what they've achieved.'

Max added, 'If people are calling us the next JLS, that's cool - we'd be very happy to have their success! Our music's really different though. They've gone down a more R&B route, whereas we're more indie.' But Siva sums it up perfectly: 'To be even mentioned in the same breath as JLS is a compliment.'

Since February 2010, the lads have been working with the likes of Guy Chambers, Taio Cruz, Steve Mac and Cathy Dennis on songs for the album, which the boys promise will be a stunning of mix of tracks. So far they have recorded around fifty songs, half of which they have co-written themselves.

'Most of them are pretty upbeat,' Max has revealed. 'But there will be a couple of slow ones for the girls, and there's one ['Let's Get Ugly'] with a sound clip from a Clint Eastwood film [*The Good, The Bad and the Ugly*] that the older generation might recognize.'

Of all the songs so far, debut single 'All Time Low', written by Westlife scribes Steve Mac and Wayne Hector, is the lads' favourite. 'That songs really nails what we're about as a band,' Max explained. 'I love the way it just starts with a vocal and a few strings, and then it just builds and builds to this massive sound.'

The boys also explain that working with such pop luminaries as Guy Chambers has been amazing. 'Working with someone like Guy was pretty daunting at first, he's a bit of legend isn't he?' Siva gushes. 'He was the first person we worked with in the studio, ever, when we started on the album. He just sat us in a room and he said, "OK, sing!" and we had to sing a song he gave us. It was just surreal. I think we can agree, we were all bricking it.'

'Guy's such a nice guy, though,' Tom says of Chambers. 'We were all a bit like, "It's the guy who wrote Angels!" It took a couple of days for us to get to know him, but he's so down to earth, I've never met a guy like him. He rode up on his bike one morning; he'd had a few beers the night before, and he was chatting away - and we were like, "What's he on about?" He's brilliant. He throws the best parties, too!'

One of the tracks that Guy has worked on is the kooky tune 'Let's Get Ugly', which samples Ennio Morricone. And its boundary-pushing sound has made a big impact on the boys. 'I love that track – that's actually where we got the name The Wanted from. Nathan came up with it,' says Tom. 'It came out of the whole Wild West vibe of that song, and just sounds cool, not too cheesy.'

With the album due out in shops in November 2010, the boys are preparing to take on the the likes of Take That, JLS and Joe McElderry, who also have albums out around the same time. But the fellas say they aren't going to be shaking in their boots and will remain calm.

'We just have to do our own thing,' Max says. '*The X Factor*'s huge and Take That are leagues ahead of us. We just do what we do and worry about ourselves rather than anyone else. Simon Cowell is one of the most powerful men in music so fair play to them if they've got a deal with him and get to perform on *The X Factor*. I watch it, I buzz off it, me. If we had the opportunity to go on it that'd be amazing but until we do we'll just stick to our guns.'

The future of The Wanted: What The Experts Say

Natalie Edwards Tabloid journalist
(*Daily Star, Sunday Mirror*)

What did you make of the band when you first heard their song?
I have to confess I wasn't a fan to start with, as I thought they might be cheesy and not as cool as JLS. But after I heard 'All Time Low', I grew to really like them. Then once I met them I knew straightaway that they were a top bunch of lads.

Who was your favourite member and why?
Before meeting them, I would have said Max because he's got the classic boyband looks and is a cheeky chappie. But after meeting them I really like Jay, too. Although he's not your stereotypical boyband looker, he is really funny and a good joker.

What do you think makes them different from other boybands?
I think the fact that they don't look put together. I guess it's a bit like the male version of The Spice Girls: they all have very different personalities, and they're not all slick like JLS. I'm not sure if there can be a new kind of boyband - they are all essentially doing the same stuff and appealing to the same fans. But they definitely seem a bit more individual than the manufactured bands.

How do you think they compare to JLS? Should JLS be worried?
I don't think JLS should be worried just yet since they've got several number ones and BRITS under their designer belts. But it will definitely be interesting to see if The Wanted can rival them later down the line. I'm hoping they will bring back 90's boyband mania. Yum.

How successful do you think they will be?
It's hard to say as I haven't heard the rest of their material, but I would like to say they will be around

for several years and have their own headline arena shows like JLS have succeeded in doing.

Which member is the one likely to be the most famous or most popular with the fans?
Definitely Max. Probably Nathan too, as he'll be a boyband version of Justin Bieber for the fans.

Do you think they have a good team behind them?
Yep, they definitely seem to have a very good PR campaign and team behind them. They've obv got the same peeps as Girls Aloud and JLS, and that looks to have worked out by getting them to No 1 without hardly any national radio plays.

You've met them... What are they really like?
They were top lads when I met them - so much personality, joking around and they were very, very flirty. Perfect combination. Definitely very charming guys and this will get them far.

Cristo Foufas, Lbc Radio Dj

What did you think of them when you first heard them?
I thought the song sounded great – very cool, really catchy with great lyrics. It sounds pretty different to most other boybands around so that should stand them in good stead.

Who is your favourite The Wanted member?
They all have their own special qualities, but I think Max is my favourite, as I have met him once and he was so friendly. And he's the best looking of them all.

Do you think they are different to the usual boybands we've seen?
Well, they seem a lot more edgy than the likes of Westlife and Boyzone. They seem really original. They haven't been formed on a TV talent show, and haven't just given us boring love songs.

Do you think JLS should be quaking in their designer boots?

Yes, I think they should be very worried as The Wanted are far cooler and didn't need The X Factor to get famous. I think the songs might be a lot cooler too. It'll be interesting to see how the two bands square up to each other over the next few months. I think they could actually be as successful as Take That if the songs are good. They could be around for a while because the vibe about them is good, the whole industry are talking about them, and the company that manage them have such big plans.

Sarah Smith, from Same Difference

What did you make of the band when you first heard their song?
I thought they were just brilliant when I first saw them. 'All Time Low' was brilliant and really catchy!

Who's your favourite member?
It has to be Jay, because when I met him he was a really nice lad, and gorgeous looking too!

What do you think makes them different from other boybands?
I think that they are a lot more approachable than other boybands. They seem like guys who could be your best friend.

How do you think they compare to JLS? Should they be worried?
I think that both bands are as good as each other. I think that The Wanted are better singers, but JLS are better dancers so they both have pluses and minuses! I think JLS will have to get used to sharing their fans!

How successful do you think they will be?
I think that The Wanted could be huge if they keep on working hard and producing brilliant songs! They also have a great team behind them and they seem like great lads.

Which member is the one likely to be the most popular with the fans?
I think that Nathan will be the most popular with the younger fans, as he is the youngest member of the band! I think that Siva and Jay will be the most popular with the women!

Are The Wanted a new kind of boyband, or just the same old same old?
I think that The Wanted are very much like the boybands of the 90s, and this is a great thing! There is something for everyone and they have fab songs!

If you have met them, what were they like?
I have met Jay and he is a really friendly guy and such a nice person. We have been on lots of shows with them but have never seen them properly but I would

love to sit down with them and have a catch up! We always hear how lovely they are from everyone we meet!

Geraint Humphries (WeArePopSlags.com)

What do you make of The Wanted?
When we first heard about them we were really excited to hear a new boyband with great songs; JLS need some competition!

Who's your favourite member?
It's a toss-up between Siva and Max. We love Siva's exotic looks, but Max's hotness simply cannot be denied. Plus we love his gruff northern tones!

What do you think makes them different to most boybands?
They have personalities. They are a bit more rough and tumble than boybands of yore. They seem like a great bunch of boys who know how to have a good time and aren't frightened of a little bit of naughtiness!

Should JLS be worried?
There is room for both groups. JLS have the moves, but The Wanted have the advantage of being the new boys on the block. It'll be good to see the two of them

taking each other on in the charts. With their debut single rocketing to number one, we think the sky is the limit for these boys.

Who do you think will become the most popular?
Max, I think, because he does the most interviews and is therefore the most visible. He seems to be the unofficial frontman. But they all have something fun about them. So it could be Jay, as he's funny, or Nathan, because he's cute, or Tom, because he's a bit mouthy and a bit of a lad! To be honest, there's a boy in there for everyone.

Angela Murray, fan, aged fifteen

What did you make of the band when you first heard their song?
When I first heard the song, I thought it was amazing. It sounded really cool. And it had a great beat and a catchy tune. I also liked the boys' voices. Max's is my favourite because it's all growly.

Who was your favourite member and why?
I liked them all but all in different ways. Jay is cute and so funny. I like his hair – it's really cool, and I like the fact he's so funny. Then I like Nathan because he is so sweet and he has a nice smile. Tom is really cheeky and he always makes me laugh. I think he would be fun to hang out with. Max is really good-looking. I love his shaved head. I can see him being the popular one and I love his voice too. Siva is just amazing to look at. He is so handsome and I love his Irish accent. It's just so sexy. I love the fact he has a twin. Can you imagine two of them?

What do you think makes them different from other boybands?
They're not cheesy like some boybands. The music is really good – a bit rocky, a bit indie, a bit dancey. They sound a lot different to bands like West Life and JLS.

How do you think they compare to JLS? Should JLS be worried?
I think they're much hotter than JLS! Sorry Marvin, JB, Aston and Oritsé! I think their voices are better too. I think JLS should be very scared because The Wanted are just so good. But then they are also both so different, so there's room for both, I guess.

How successful do you think they will be?
I like to think they will be very successful. If the songs are as good as 'All Time Low' and 'Heart Vacancy', then they can't go to wrong.

Which member is the one likely to be the most popular with the fans?
For me, I love Max. He's gorgeous, he's fit and he's

got a great voice. But they're all cute in their own way.

Have you met them? What are they really like?
I met them at a signing in Nottingham. I queued up for hours, but it was worth the wait. They were so nice and friendly and funny. They told me they liked my hair. They are so cool, and so good to their fans. They're the best pop band around.

Boybands That Everyone Should Know About

The Wanted are the latest in a long line of boybands that have danced their way into the charts and into our hearts. Some have been great, some not so good, but nevertheless they have all left a little mark behind them.

Here, we take a look back at some of the most memorable boybands of the past twenty years and look forward to some new ones that could be nipping at The Wanted's heels…

Take That

While most of you will know Gary Barlow, Mark Owen, Howard Donald and Jason Orange for their hit singles 'Patience', 'Shine' and 'Rule The World', Take That actually have been around for a lot longer than you might think. They were formed in 1990 along with a fith member, Robbie Williams, and released their first single, 'Do What You Like' later that same year. Unfortunately, it failed to make the Top 75, even though it was accompanied by a saucy video which saw all the gorgeous boys totally naked and lying in jelly. The band really started to make an impact when they released a cover of Tavares track 'It only Takes A Minute'. Hit after hit followed, with 'Could It Be Magic', fronted by then band member, Robbie Williams providing them with their first top five hit. Their second album *Everything Changes* spawned four number ones – 'Pray', 'Relight My Fire', 'Babe' and the title track, 'Everything Changes'. In July 1995, the boys released their third album *Nobody Else*, which featured the very popular 'Back For Good', which introduced an older fanbase to the group. But disaster struck when funnyman Robbie quit the band, saying he wanted to go solo. It would later emerge that the rest of the boys weren't happy with Robbie's lack of commitment to the band, and suggested they part company. After a tour as a fourpiece, Take That announced they were splitting. Over the next few years, Gary Barlow, the band's lead singer and songwriter tried to go solo, but fell flat on his face, as did the cute one from the band, Mark Owen, who released a string of moderately successful indie-flavoured albums. In 2006, Take That announced that they were reuniting and returned with a string of grown-up hits. In 2010, Take That buried the hatchet with newly-married Robbie Williams and recorded a one off album with him.

Fit rating: 8/10 Back in the day, Mark was the cute one and Howard the body. These days, Gary's now the hottest in the band, Jason looks supercool while Robbie's not looking too shabby either.

Albums:
Take That And Party (1993)
Everything Changes (1994)
Nobody Else (1995)
Beautiful World (2006)
The Circus (2008)

Best Known For: Flashing their bums in the 'Do What You Like' vid, Robbie quitting at their height, their amazing comeback

Listen to: 'Do What You Like', 'Once You've Tasted Love', 'Pray', 'Relight My Fire', 'Could It Be Magic', 'Back For Good', 'Rule The World', 'Meaning Of Love', 'Babe'

East 17

If Take That were the goody two shoes of nineties boybands, then East 17 were the bad boys from hell. Hailing from Walthamstow in the east of London, the group, comprising of Tony Mortimer, Terry Coldwell, John Hendy and lead vocalist Brian Harvey, provided pop fans with a meaty alternative to Take That's squeaky clean brand of pop. With hits like 'Deep', 'House Of Love' and 'Gold', they fast became pin-ups. However, it was the uncharacteristically cute ballad 'Stay Another Day', which gave them their first number one. After a bust up over some silly comments Brian made on the radio, the band became a three piece. They have subsequently tried to make a comeback, but it never was as successful as that of their biggest rivals Take That!

Fit rating: 6/10 Not exactly beaten with the ugly stick, but nowhere near as cute as Take That or The Wanted boys. But if you like boys with a cheeky glint in their eyes, this lot are for you.

Albums:
Walthamstow (1993)
Steam (1994)
Up All Night (1996)

Best Known For: Brian Harvey's dodgy headwear (think Dappy from N Dubz), slating Take That, Brian being kicked out of the band for saying stupid things.

Listen to: 'Gold', 'Deep', 'Steam', 'Around The World', 'Do You Still', 'It's Alright', 'Stay Another Day', 'Hold my Body Tight', 'Someone To Love'

Ant & Dec

These days, these Geordie fellas are best known as TV presenters of *Saturday Night Take Away* and *Britain's Got Talent*, but not so long ago they were tearing up the charts with a bunch of joyous pop tunes. Starting out as actors on teen soap *Biker Grove*, the pair found pop fame when their characters, PJ & Duncan, recorded a song in the show. The track, 'Tonight I'm Free', barely dented the charts when it was released in reality, but their follow up 'Let's Get Ready To Rhumble', proved a lot more successful and gave them a tip ten hit. A string of hit records followed, including the beautiful ballad 'Perfect', the dancetastic 'When I Fall In Love', and the supercool 'Shout'. The wacky duo – think of a less bouncy, Geordie Jedward, and you might get an idea of what they were like – were so popular with fans that they even toured the country. Eventually, they packed in the pop lark and went on to become TV legends, starting out on *SM:TV* and *CD:UK* and ending up on smash hit show *Britain's Got Talent*.

Fit rating: 7/10 Hard to choose between them, as most girls fall into either Camp Dec or Camp Ant. Both equally as cute as each other, but in a totally different way and appealing to different kinds of girls. They might not have been pumped up with muscles, but they were funny. And who doesn't love a funny guy?

Albums:
Psyche (1994)
Top Katz (1995)
The Cult Of Ant & Dec (1997)

Best Known For: Ant as PJ blinded in a paint ball accident, 'Let's Get Ready To Rhumble' and shaving a young child's hair off on their TV show.

Listen to: 'If I Give You My Number', 'Stuck On You', 'When I Fall In Love', 'Perfect', 'Shout', 'You Krazy Katz', 'Gonna B Alright', 'Always My Love'

Westlife

If you like your boybands to sing drippy ballads that pull tenderly at your heartstrings, then Westlife are your boys. Known primarily for sitting on stools and then standing up for the key change as the song swirls to its climax, the band, who are managed by Louis Walsh from *The X Factor*, have gone on to carve out an eleven year career with songs that are most certainly pleasant to the ear, but probably more the kind of easy listening your mum does the washing to. But even though the boys look like squeaky clean fellas, former band member, Brian McFadden did the dirty on his then wife Kerry Katona on his stag night, and later with the band and then his wife. Meanwhile, hunky Mark Feehily disappointed his female fans when he revealed he liked boys instead. Sadly, the other boys; Kian Egan, Nicky Byrne and Shane Filan, are all loved up and married.

Fit rating: 9/10 They might have been around for over ten years, but these fellas are still fitties. If you like your dark brooding types, you have gorgeous

Shane and Mark, but for lovers of blonde guys, you have sexy Nicky and cute Kian.

Albums:
Westlife (1999)
Coast To Coast (2000)
World Of Our Own (2001)
Turn Around (2003)
Allow Us To Be Frank (2004)
Face To face (2005)
Back Home (2007)
Where We Are (2009)

Best Known For: Their stool dance, ballads, covers and their irritating reluctance to either dance or flash their torsos.

Listen to: 'I have A Dream', 'My Love', 'Soledad', 'Open Your Heart', 'You light Up My Life', 'Mandy', 'Flying Without Wings', 'Home', 'Fool Again', 'Seasons Of The Sun'

Boyzone

Before Westlife was a spark in Louis Walsh's eye, he dreamt up Boyzone; a group of fit lads who loved to croon a ballad. And croon away they did, offering us up tunes like 'Baby Can I Hold You tonight', 'Father and Son', 'Words' and 'No Matter What'. Occasionally they tried an upbeat number like 'Picture of You' and 'When the Going Gets Tough'. But the hardcore fans loved to hear Ronan Keating's growling vocals as he banged out those ballads. During a break away from each other, Ronan released a few solo records, including 'When You say Nothing At all', realized he rather like the solo life and stayed clear of the band for a few years. Meanwhile, Stephen, who had revealed he rather liked boys, married his partner Andrew, but sadly failed as a solo star and went into musicals instead. Burly Keith Duffy tried his hand at acting in *Coronation Street,* while Mikey Graham suffered from depression. In 2008, the boys all reunited, but were rocked when Stephen sadly passed away in 2009. Meanwhile, Ronan and his wife of ten years broke up. Now the band remain a four piece, and released their album *Brother* in 2010.

Fit rating: 5/10 Even though they were in their early twenties, four of the lads looked like they were twice the age. Ronan was the main cutie, looking boyish to start with, then rather manly as the years went by. Handsome Shane Lynch drastically changed his looks over the years, and decorated his body with one too many tattoos.

Albums:
Said And Done (1995)
A Different Beat (1997)
Where We Belong (1998)
By Request (1999)
Brother (2010)

Best known for: Their covers. Ronan Keating, hits 'Life Is A Roller Coaster' and 'When You Say Nothing At All'

Listen to: 'Love Me For Me A Reason', 'So Good', 'Father And Son', 'Words', 'No Matter What', 'Coming Home Now', 'Isn't It A Wonder'

JLS

Sexy four piece who came second on *The X Factor* behind Alexandra Burke. Despite that, they went on to have a string of number one singles, including 'Everybody in Love', 'The Club Is Alive' and 'Beat Again'. In just a short year they have captured the hearts of the nation. Wherever they go, the girls are sure to follow and when they do, there's chaos. Marvin broke his fans' hearts when he started dating Rochelle from the Saturdays, and Aston has been linked to all manner of girls. In autumn 2010, the fellas take on The Wanted when their second album hits the stores. Will they outclass our favourite boys? We'll have to wait and see.

Fit rating: 9/10 What can you say about these boys? They are fit, fit, fit, fit. Marvin is the sexiest of the four, though Aston's weeny muscled body is enough to get girls all excited.

Albums:
JLS (2009)

Best known for: Flashing their six packs, Marvin's womanly tops, tight dance moves, Marvin dating Rochelle, starring on *The X Factor*.

Listen to: 'Everybody In Love', 'The Club Is Alive', 'One Shot', 'Kickstart', 'Don't Go', 'Beat Again'

Five

Five sexy lads with muscles and piercings, called Abs, J, Richie, Scott and Sean. They declared that they were five bad boys with the power to rock us. They were a bit rougher and tougher than the average boyband and the nation fell in love with them after they stormed the charts with a bunch of pop crackers like 'Let's Dance', 'Everybody Get Up', 'Keep On Movin' and 'If Ya Gettin Down'. After three albums, they called time on the band when Sean disappeared. Abs tried to go solo, but failed to match the heady heights of Five, meanwhile, J tried to revive his career by appearing on *I'm A Celebrity Get Me Out Of Here*.

Fit Rating: 9/10 With J's beefy bod and Ab's lithe physique and Richie's dazzling eyes, there were enough Fitty McFits in this combo!

Albums:
5ive (1998)
Invincible (1999)
Kingsize (2001)
Let's Dance (2002)

Best known for: Ab's weird Rastafarian accent, Richie's eyes, J's vests and Sean not saying much, Sean's cardboard cut out in the 'Let's Dance' Video.

Listen to: 'Keep On Movin', 'If Ya Gettin Down', 'Let's Dance', 'Everybody Get Up'

Who Will Rival The Wanted?

The Wanted might be the latest boyband off the blocks, but nipping at their heels are a whole host of wannabe heartthrobs. But do our fave fivesome have anything to worry about?

Jedward

You know these two; they're John and Edward Grimes. They're the wacky Irish fellas who irritated Simon Cowell on *The X Factor* with their dodgy singing and crazy dance routines. Despite audiences booing them throughout the series, they have gone on to release an album full of tracks and have had their own TV show.

Find out more at planetjedward.com

Fit rating: 8/10

Chance of success: Mission Accomplished!

Kaos Theory

You may have seen these four lads on the recent Westlife and Girls Aloud tours. Check out www.myspace.com/kaostheoryofficial to hear their song 'Drop Me Off' and you will also see that the boys – which include a Pop Idol reject called Chris – are all pretty fit fellas. Need to hear more to see if The Wanted should be The Worried.

Fit Rating: 9/10

Chance of success: Classy video, great song. Very likely indeed.

IBoy Banned

Four kind-of-cute lads who specialise in Hi-NRG pop who have toured Europe. Check out their slow 'Street Lights', it's quite a catchy tunette! Find out more about them at www.boybanned.com

Fit rating: 5/10

Chance of success: If 'Street Lights' is an indicator of what they can offer, then they could be pretty cool!

The WANTED

Max George,

Siva Kaneswaran,

Tom Parker,

Nathan Sykes

and James McGuiness.